Sign Language & Farm Animals

Bela Davis

Abdo Kids Junior
is an Imprint of Abdo Kids
abdobooks.com

Abdo
EVERYDAY SIGN LANGUAGE
Kids

abdobooks.com

Published by Abdo Kids, a division of ABDO, P.O. Box 398166, Minneapolis, Minnesota 55439.

Printed in the United States of America, North Mankato, Minnesota.

102024

012025

THIS BOOK CONTAINS RECYCLED MATERIALS

Photo Credits: Shutterstock

Production Contributors: Teddy Borth, Jennie Forsberg, Grace Hansen

Design Contributors: Candice Keimig, Pakou Moua

Library of Congress Control Number: 2024936606

Publisher's Cataloging-in-Publication Data

Names: Davis, Bela, author.

Title: Sign language & farm animals / by Bela Davis

Description: Minneapolis, Minnesota : Abdo Kids, 2025 | Series: Everyday sign language set 3 | Includes online resources and index.

Identifiers: ISBN 9798384902768 (lib. bdg.) | ISBN 9798384903468 (ebook) | ISBN 9798384903819 (Read-to-me ebook)

Subjects: LCSH: American Sign Language--Juvenile literature. | Domestic animals--Juvenile literature. | Deaf--Means of communication--Juvenile literature. | Language acquisition--Juvenile literature.

Classification: DDC 419--dc23

Table of Contents

Signs and Farm Animals

ASL is a visual language. There is a sign for all your favorite farm animals!

FARM

1. Make an open hand
2. Bring thumb to the opposite jaw (for example, the right thumb would touch the left jaw)
3. Slide thumb from one side of the jaw to the other

Cows on a farm

graze in the fields.

COW

1. Make the “Y” sign
2. Touch thumb to the side of the forehead
3. Twist forward at the wrist a few times

Sheep stay together in flocks.

SHEEP

1. Hold one hand in front of the body, palm down
2. Make the "V" sign with the other hand
3. Turn the "V" hand upside down
4. Move the "V" hand up the arm while making a clipping motion, as if sheering a sheep!

Baby goats stay
near their mom.

GOAT

1. Make a bent "V" sign or a loose fist
2. With the palm facing inward, tap hand to the chin
3. Then tap the hand to the forehead ending in a "V" hand

Pigs roll in mud
to keep cool.

PIG

1. Bring one open hand up under the chin, palm facing down
2. Tuck and open the fingers a couple of times

A fence keeps donkeys safe.

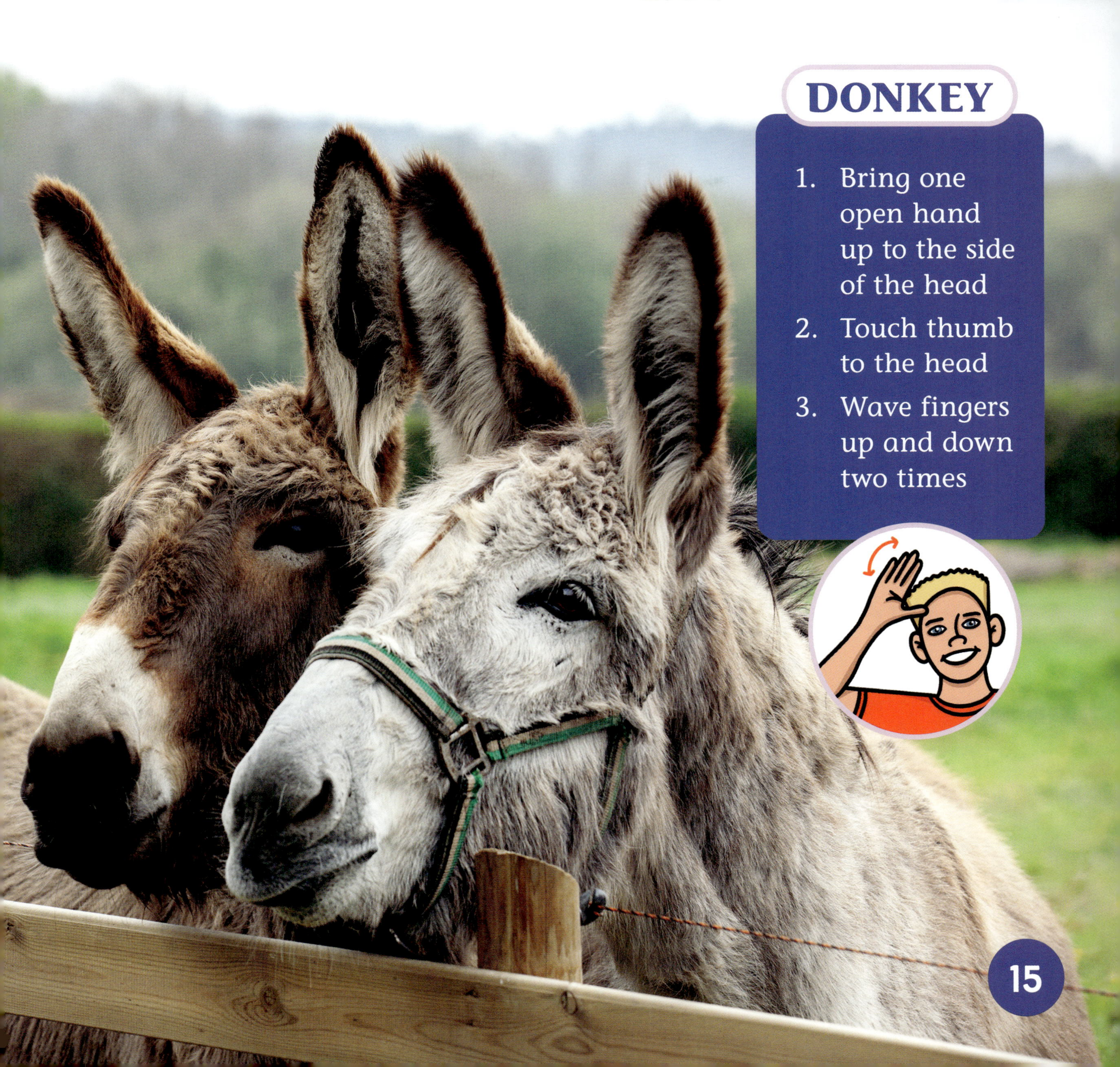

DONKEY

1. Bring one open hand up to the side of the head
2. Touch thumb to the head
3. Wave fingers up and down two times

Roosters **crow** just before sunrise.

ROOSTER

1. Make a "3" hand
2. Tap forehead twice with the tip of the thumb

Chickens can lay up to one egg a day.

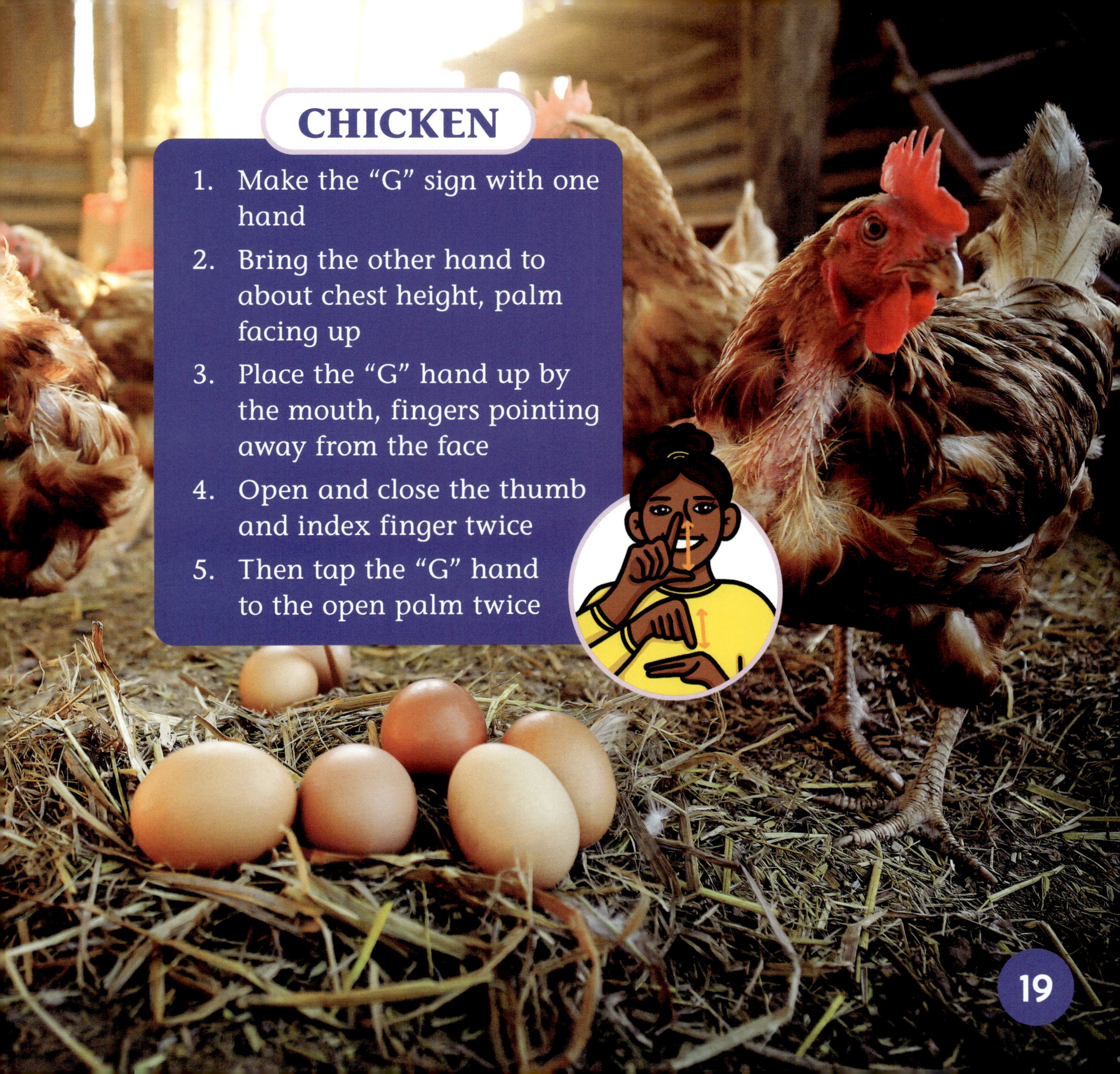

CHICKEN

1. Make the "G" sign with one hand
2. Bring the other hand to about chest height, palm facing up
3. Place the "G" hand up by the mouth, fingers pointing away from the face
4. Open and close the thumb and index finger twice
5. Then tap the "G" hand to the open palm twice

Ducks keep gardens on the farm clean by eating bugs.

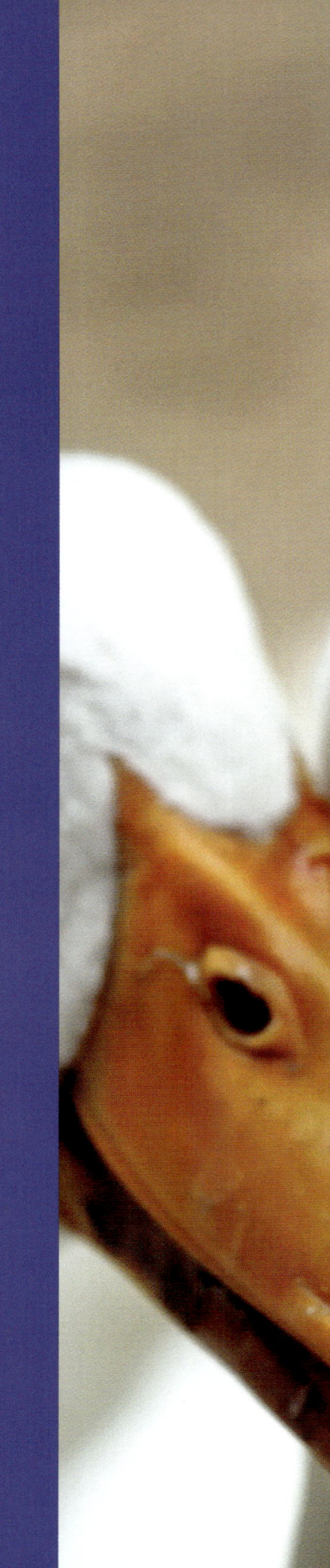

DUCK

1. Extend the middle and index fingers and thumb out while tucking the other fingers in
2. The middle and index fingers should be touching
3. Place hand up by the mouth
4. Close and open the index and middle fingers and thumb a couple of times

The ASL Alphabet!

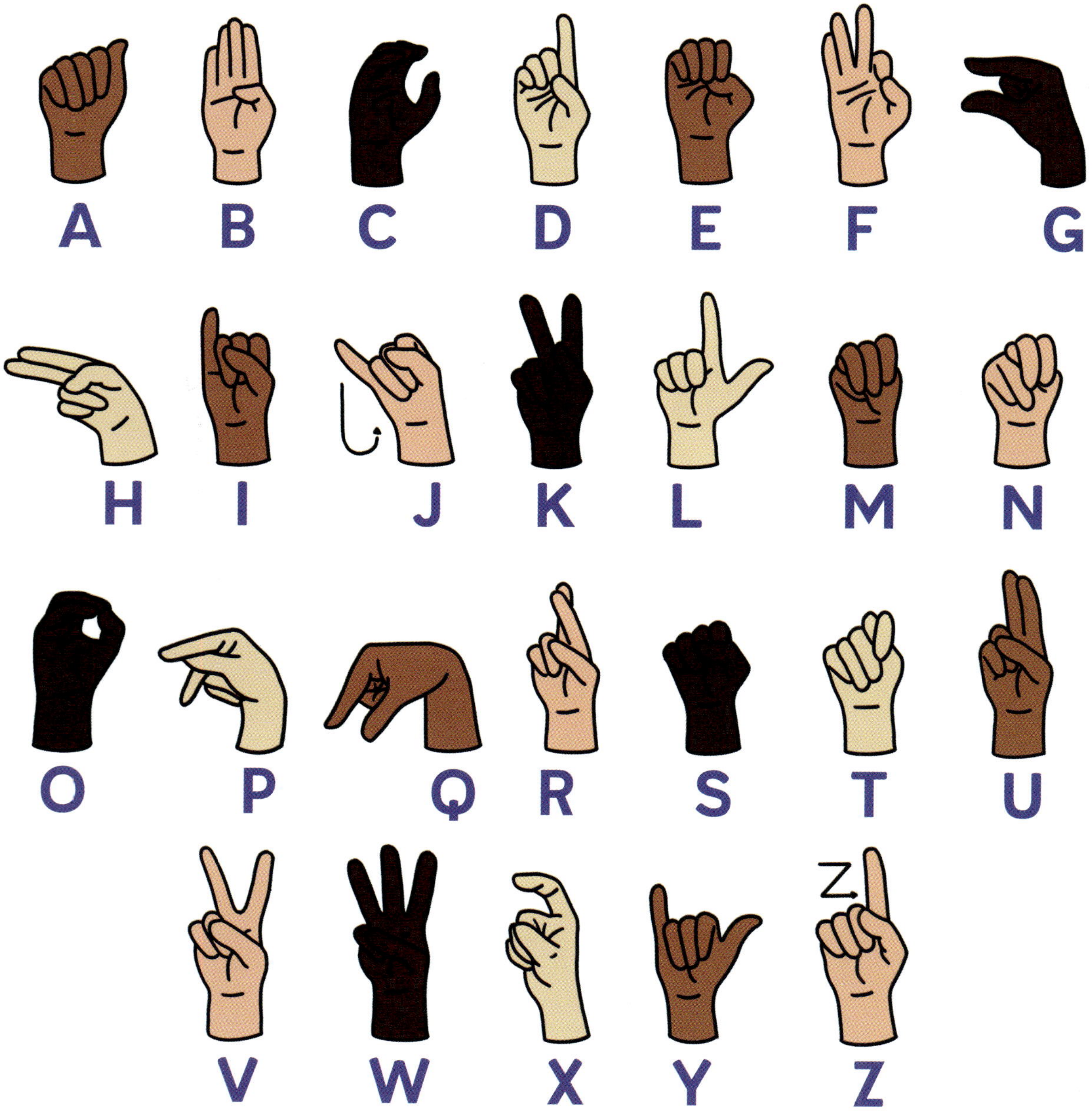

A B C D E F G

H I J K L M N

O P Q R S T U

V W X Y Z

Glossary

ASL
short for American Sign Language, a language used by many deaf people in North America.

crow
to make the harsh cry of a rooster.

graze
to feed on growing grass.

Index

Visit **abdokids.com** to access crafts, games, videos, and more!

Use Abdo Kids code

ESK2768

or scan this QR code!